Stream, Pebbles, Leaves

Art Bell

Lexingford Publishing Series in Poetry

ISBN 978-0-9859480-1-6

www.lexingfordpublishing.yolasite.com

Lexingford Publishing Series in Poetry

Lexingford Publishing

New York

Preface

Poems, like the weather, defy prediction, explanation, and origin. I cannot add helpful commentary on the where's, when's, and why's of these works.

What I can say, in candor, is that Wordsworth's definition of a poet—"a man speaking to men"— has occurred to me often in the act of writing. I have also imagined, if not achieved, Walter Pater's great defense for art as an opportunity "to burn always with this hard, gem-like flame, to maintain this ecstasy."

I dedicate this collection with love to my youngest daughter Madeleine, a poet herself; she reminded me to write often and to try to write well.

Art Bell

Colton, New York

January 22, 2015

A Poem a Week

If a poem could be born each week

I wonder

If it would need special care,

A nursery of the soul

Where it can sleep and grow

Under watchful eyes?

Or would it roar upon us

Like a headline

Dragging urgent clothing

Thrown on for the quick trip

From mind to mind?

A fair question. I would guess

A poem would not rest long

In a quiet cradle within the mind.

A poem would reach for rags

And scream its name,

Even to an incubated world.

The Guest

The guest was particularly taken

By the rocks, she said.

Their size (my God).

Their age (who knows?)

What stories they could tell

If they had mouths.

"There, that one!" and

"The biggest yet!", her exclamations

On an afternoon excursion.

If we aspire to be what we admire,

Perhaps the guest wished herself a rock,

Imposing, immovable,

Bulwarked against time

Like a dam against water.

What stories she could tell,

Of change, decay, seasons,

Loss. Loveliness.

My guest a rock, silent sentinel

To ages as they passed--

A rock too strong to change

Or hear or see or feel.

What stories she could not tell.

Mars

I am off to Mars,

Cinched in with fertile men and women

Who will descend, scratch the red earth, no, mars,

Beneath their hamster-tube environment

And say, "Let's reproduce."

"Let's make Martians,

Self-sufficient and robust,

Since help is months away at best,

And we must do for ourselves."

"Let's remember to forget

That tiny blue dot in our red sky

And focus instead on the freedom

Of doing things

In our own Martian way,

Whatever those turn out to be."

"Let's make new words

For the umeixo we excavated

Four sectomines ago,

A rare discovery indeed

For a planet thought dead."

"Let's be chary

In our sporadic communications

With the old world,

Suffering as it does

With heat and filth

And people, people, people

Who did not choose

To start anew on Mars."

"In time, we will no doubt

Contract a virus, harmless here,

But lethal if returned to Earth.

We will then be feared

And not invited back

Like Marco Polo's

To tell our tales

Around the fires

Of home no longer home."

"When Earth looks up

On the rare unpolluted night

At the red planet

Twinkling pure and bright

And wonders how we fare,

We will not respond.

We will not remake Mars

In Earth's image."

Walloween

On Walloween

The wittle witchies beg for

Wandy, crying

"Wick or wheat!"

Not in fact expecting weal wheat

Which I wrap like wandy.

They wonder what a wad

Of wheat is wooing

In their wags of wicky wandy.

They woll it wound in their wingers,

Wasking one another "Will we wheat it

Or whoa it away?"

It doesn't wook or waste like wandy.

But they wheat it anyway,

Weasoning that this must be the wick

In "wick or wheat!" and must be wallowed.

It wells and weals like wed

Or wackers.

"We weight it!" they wail

And wit it wout,

"Wick or wandy," they wail,

"No wheat, no whey."

Dinner Party

The dinner party

Was integral to business

The following day

And therefore

Had to come off

Smashingly.

Before our guests arrived

We reminded one another

Of don'ts we might otherwise do:

Don't eat with your fingers.

Don't spit out bad food.

Don't blow your nose on your napkin.

Don't screech your fork against the plate.

Don't steal food from others.

Don't discuss how or if you bathe.

Don't discuss shaving.

Don't inquire about religion.

Don't confirm, deny, or mention sex.

We set the table,

Sure that we had not only

Prepared the food

But had also prepared ourselves

For polite company.

Parts

When my hand fell off

I stuffed it into my pocket

To keep it dry and warm.

When my foot fell off

I tucked it into an old slipper

In the corner of my closet.

I was less careful with my nose.

One day it rolled softly down my chest,

Through my legs,

And onto the sidewalk.

This was the nose that a girlfriend

Had called quite large for my face.

The word 'schnozz' had appeared more than once

On my Facebook page.

So I let it go.

Some eagle-eyed walker will no doubt find it,

Express disgust,

And turn it in to the Missing Persons Department.

The police notes will read,

"An anonymous nose missing its person."

Lacking a foot, a hand, and a generally unpopular nose,

I found a cane a necessity.

Assisted in this way, I saw a doctor,

Who proclaimed my malady

Non-life-threatening, though frustrating.

He prescribed a liquid medicine—

"Drops," he joked.

They didn't save my head,

Which began to slip and jostle,

Eventually tumbling into my lap

As I watched re-runs of Lucy.

I knew enough to keep my head,

God knows,

And rigged a frontal back-pack,

With holes cut out for eyes and mouth

(The nose, you will recall,

Being no longer in play.)

I could now resume my daily life.

My eyes still twinkled, I was told,

My mouth still capable of

An occasional belly laugh.

In all the ways that mattered,

I was my old self.

Restaurants posed a problem,

Needless to say,

As I dribbled coffee into

The esophageal hole between my shoulders.

Adults tended to flee these moments,

But their children remained behind,

Urging me to play the tinman

And use my funnel,

Which in fact I did,

Not only for their enjoyment,

But also to ingest

A well-mashed soufflé or boiled egg.

My ears fell too, like autumn leaves,

As did my butt,

Which I found one morning

In a leg of my pajamas.

I must say I was taken aback.

As for final arrangements,

Should my torso itself snap apart

Despite my doctor's drops,

I have directed that I be buried whole,

My parts collected (except for the objectionable nose)

And placed in one grave,

Lest my legacy be one of littering.

I hope to see my Maker chest to face,

A being created in His image

And, in passing, most eager to know

If He feels a suspicious loosening

In the joints of His mighty knees

Or a giant toe starting to flop

Out of place as He cinches His sandals

For another day of keeping things together.

What Lies Immediately Ahead

In every poem

Words crawl across the page

Like ants in a row,

Each following each by some dim scent

Of what lies immediately ahead.

Day and night they do their patient work,

Black moving across white in orderly precision

Without guide or guard to keep them straight.

Only the last word on the page

Pops into the anthill of the mind

To join thousands, thousands

Of fellow workers there.

Except when the last word stops

Before the hole,

Freezing the entire line behind,

Halting the movement of the mind,

Reducing all

To just words on the page.

The Person at the Other End

The world is missing parts.

Not enough water in the desert.

Not enough ice at the poles.

Not enough trees in the rain forest.

The world did not lose these parts.

It has no mind. It has no will.

But language comes from mind and will.

When it misses parts

There is a reason.

Consider: a pitcher has a catcher.

A preacher has a flock.

A teacher has her students.

And a caller has . . .

Ah, the missing part.

What does the caller have?

A callee? Certainly not.

A receiver? No.

A billion calls each day

And no one knows

Exactly what to call

The person at the other end.

Language has a mind and will.

Parts do not go missing

By accident.

We choose not to know

What to call

The one

Who says

"Hello?"

Lighthouse

Living in a lighthouse

As I do for the summer,

A certain decorum is expected

But not maintained

By my fraternity brothers

And their pack of friends,

Who spread lawnchairs willy-nilly

Round the grounds

And souse themselves

On tequila shots and cheap rum.

They name their drinks, irreverently,

For local shipwrecks:

"Bounty of the Seas,"

"Columbia Forever,"

"Pacific Zephyr,"

"Asia Unsinkable,"

And other hulks now

Rotting out beyond

The jagged shoals,

A mile of hidden rock

Now marked for one and all

By the lighthouse.

Ships cannot see my friends,

The mist obscuring

Lawnchairs, pig, and rum.

Ships see only the pulsing light,

Telling craft large and small

They are well positioned

Far enough offshore

For safe passage

To southern ports.

Ships do not complain about my friends.

No, it is the tourists,

Each of whom spent six dollars

To walk the winding downward path

Along the coastal ridge

To the lighthouse point.

Even their ten-year-olds say

"What the hell?"

When they come upon

Twenty or so revelers

Roasting a spitted pig

And swigging grog.

Is someone watching the beacon,

Should it need immediate repair?

Is the lighthouse even occupied

By a responsible party?

Where exactly is the man or woman

Paid to stand guard over lives at sea,

Dependent as they are

On the steady throb of light

Piercing fog a hundred miles

In the dark?

These are the questions of parents,

Asked of no one in particular.

And where is the lighthouse keeper,

Presumably part of our six dollar fee?

He is basting the pig,

With glazed eyes and sweaty brow

(keeper and pig).

One tourist interrupts the fete

To say the beacon is no doubt

Automatic

Or under satellite control

And really needs no

Human help.

"No," the keeper or someone

Who can still form words

Says, "No, it can go out at any time."

The revelers laugh at the confusion

Of the tourists.

"And what would happen if . . ." begins

A serious tall man among the tourists,

Who has paid not only for himself

But also for his wife and four children.

"What if the light went out right now?"

"We don't know!" squeal the drunkards,

Slathering the skewered pig

With more alcohol than sauce.

"We don't know!" they chant,

Natives around an ancient fire.

By ones and twos, then all together,

The tourists retreat up

The quarter-mile path

To the paved lot

Provided as part of their fee.

Some resolve to call their senators.

Others check the calendar

To see if they had stumbled on

Some long forgotten

Bacchanalian lighthouse holiday.

"At least the light is shining,"

Parents tell their children.

"It must be automatic," repeats one father

To another.

But in fact the light I guard

Is not automatic,

Nor am I prepared to sacrifice

My pig or friends

To perform my summer job.

I believe the light will shine

Through the night

Without my care.

And should it fail,

What is to be said?

That I was found

Sprawled in stupor with friends,

Well-gnawed pork ribs all around?

What is to be said

To a container ship too near the shoals

Whose captain searched in vain

For a spot of light

Gone black?

The light probably will not fail tonight,

Nor will the pig upon the spit.

Friends will saunter off by late morning light

Resolved to do this all again

Very soon.

Next weekend, no doubt.

I guard the light, the lighthouse,

The six dollar fee,

The gravel path,

And all the rest that make

Me the designated

Summer Intern keeper

Of one of California's

Last functioning lighthouses.

I answer tourist questions

As best I can,

Being new at my job,

And understand the wide-eyed

Innocence of youth

And narrow-eyed accusations of age.

"It must be automatic,"

The father growls

As he starts his car.

The children are quiet

For a change

In the backseat,

As if in deep thought.

Leaving Home

We leave the home

For others,

Hoping it will not

Strike out at them

In all the unexpected ways

It has undone us

Through the years.

The creaking stairs

Were but a warning

Of sewer breaks

And moldy walls

And roach-infested cupboards

And leaking roof

That drips in lazy rivulets,

Against replastered walls.

We leave the home

For others, not entirely

Without guilt.

A naughty child it has been

Indeed

But not without

A shabby charm of sorts,

Despite the drafts

And wet

And heavy air.

We could not take

Our home along,

Nor did it seem

To want to come.

Others will enter

And no doubt ask

"What will we do with this?"

And "Can we cut that wall?"

And "Does the toilet even work?"

Will our home suffer

At the hands of

New owners?

A silly thought

If one credits

No emotion

To the world of sticks and rocks.

But in truth our home

Appeared to breathe,

To heave, to gasp,

To sweat at times,

And even speak

In awkward cries

Of wrenching timbers

And squealing doors.

We understood its pain

And in large part

Lived our lives

Within its walls

In companion agony,

Or, on better days,

In low-grade irritation

With the way

Things were.

We believe, therefore,

That resurrection lies

In leaving.

We turn, last boxes

Under arm, to

Glance back

At undraped windows

And locked doors.

A hinge akimbo.

A knob long missing.

We leave.

But for myself,

I must admit a certain

Place forever

In my heart

For hours spent

At dripping sinks

And days in quiet listening

To the hush of wind

Against disjointed shutters.

New owners will

Not befriend this home,

Nor will they be embraced

By its last efforts

To protect them

From winter storms

And summer rain.

They will hate this house

And, as it dies,

The house will hate them.

I see the justice

In this scheme of things,

The symmetry of abandonment

Repaid in endless, hurtful ways

Known only to the coterie

Of homes grown old.

I wonder if our home

Will remember

My regard, indeed, my love

For it through time.

I wonder if our home

Can forgive

The crystal night

In which all things changed,

In which the trusted ones

In beds and baths

Wrapped up their goods

To file in whispers

Down the walk

And out the gate.

We are bound

To another home,

One that no doubt

Has its own deep scars

And careful plan

For future

Retribution.

Appointment

The fifty minute appointment

Felt across my skin

Like a first date,

Replete with awkward silence,

Weak smiles as if

In imitation of the English Patient.

I knew enough

About psychiatry to plan

My initial sixty seconds—

The idea being, per Freud,

That doctors must not impose

A thought, a mood,

A frame of reference,

Lest the patient, moi,

Picks up the hint

And plays along.

The doctor simply

Waits

As long as it takes

For the recipient

Of psychiatric services

To say something, anything,

A launching pad

For therapeutic conversation.

I began, therefore,

With a neutral comment

Upon his office décor:

I like your primitive artwork.

Pre-Columbian? I see, but

Quite good reproductions.

He asked me

What figure in particular

Called a memory to mind.

I surveyed the room

And spotted one,

To my eye

A thick-limbed troll,

And, rising past his nose,

An enormous phallus.

What memory?

"The ice-cream man,"

I blurted, since

From my hazy youth

I recalled a vendor

Who was also

Short and thick.

"I see," the doctor said,

Making notes.

I sensed that I had

Released the race-horse in him.

No, as a child

I never knew

An ice-cream man.

Yes, of course I spent

An occasional nickel

For a treat.

I didn't know the man.

Certainly not. He

Never touched me

In that way,

Nor any of my friends.

I can't explain

Why your figurine

Recalled an ice-cream man.

I agree that it is odd.

But its meaning, doctor?

I suppose you may be right:

I may have blotted out

Ecstatic moments,

Splendor in grass,

Behind his truck.

But in truth

I don't recall at all.

Hypnotism? I doubt

That twilight sleep

Will find a crumb

Of youthful truth

That I have,

As you say,

Swept beneath the rug.

No, I am not resistant

To the technique itself.

Yes, I will be ready

When next we meet

To relax, completely,

Your voice lulling me

Toward sleepy revelation.

The fifty minutes up,

With thanks all 'round,

I leave the quiet office

Wondering if I had somehow

Tipped the balance

In my opening words

Toward ice-cream men,

Extraordinary penises, and

The remote possibility

Of an assault or sexual misadventure

In the dim recesses

Of youthful memory.

I wondered in particular

If, in my opening salvo,

I had remarked on

The fabric of the furniture,

The choice of magazines,

The slight rays of sun

Slipping warm between the drapes.

What hobby-horse

Would then be in play?

Would I be suspected

Of a sexual flavor

To my early choice

Of ice cream

A scar that somehow

Snapped my conscious mind

Like a waffle cone underfoot?

At my next visit

I am resolved

To remain silent.

Let the master make the move.

A cow does not

Approach the butcher.

Nor will I provide

The hint, the starting nudge,

That sends the doctor's mind

Reeling, whirling,

Into possibilities of exotica.

He will eventually

Ask why I am silent.

I will answer,

Truthfully,

That I am

Afraid to speak.

www.ingramcontent.com/pod-product-compliance
Lightning Source LLC
LaVergne TN
LVHW021548080426
835509LV00019B/2906